LIBRO VERITÀ

11

RICCARDO NENCINI

ORIANA FALLACI

I'll Die Standing
on My Feet

Ⴔ

EDIZIONI POLISTAMPA

1st italian edition: September 2007
1st reprint: September 2007
2nd reprint: October 2007
3rd reprint: September 2008

English Sample Edition printed in 100 copies

On the back cover:
Oriana Fallaci in the piazza at Greve in Chianti (Florence).

© 2008 Edizioni Polistampa
   Via Livorno, 8/32 - 50142 Firenze
   Tel. 055 737871 (15 lines)
   info@polistampa.com - www.polistampa.com

ISBN 978-88-596-0480-8

PUBLISHER'S NOTE

Since this intimate dialogue between Oriana and Riccardo first came out in an initial eighty thousand copies with many reprints, several events have occurred. Nencini has continued his political commitment and was elected National secretary of the PS (Socialist Party); on the eve of the second anniversary of Fallaci's death, her posthumous work *A Hat Full of Cherries* was published – the inevitable companion to this book because the city of Florence, her family and her origins are the central themes in that as well.

This edition contains small secrets that only now can be revealed. Don't ask why. I am proud to contribute with this publication towards keeping the memory of Oriana alive. I, too, have fallen under her spell as Riccardo had. Yet he had the good fortune of being her confidant and he wished to entrust the "testament" to a publishing house facing the Arno River, just like the Mannelli Tower.

Antonio Pagliai
Florence, September 2008

ORIANA FALLACI

I'll Die Standing
on My Feet

A very hot day. An unusual June, torrid like the month in 1289 that subdued the Ghibelline noblemen and knights on the Campaldino plain, on a Saturday, on St. Barnabas' day, yesterday.

I haven't seen her for four months. We have spoken to each other a few times, often by phone at night because of time zone differences. The last call was in May. Mine.

"How are you?"

"Why did you call?"

"To find out how you are."

"Just for this?" Suspicious.

"Just for this, Oriana."

Silence. A long silence.

"Thanks, Riccardo. But don't call me any more. I feel awful, really awful. The pain in my back has become unbearable and I can't see out of one eye. The cancer has spread everywhere.

Remember me as I was when you saw me the last time."

Click.

My cell phone rings non-stop in the middle of a meeting with the vice president of a Dutch region, the Gelderland. An unknown number. I excuse myself to De Vries and answer softly.

"I've been in Florence for a few days. I'd really like to see you but don't tell anyone. No one, all right? Write down this number and please call me back on Friday." I write it down and memorize it.

Friday.

A quick phone call. Short and to the point: "Come soon. I need to talk to you."

"Sunday?"

"Sunday. Alone. I don't want anyone else to see me but you. The house is small, it's like the dwarves' house in Snow White, but it's big enough for two. Take down the address."

A residential area, Cure Alte. A small green door – an English green, like the ones in the buildings of the upper middle class in London – a narrow staircase, short and steep, crowded with books, and on the other wall, etchings and lithographs. Cozy and clean rooms, a dining table for few guests and Mirella, who says goodbye and leaves. "Take your time. Call when you've finished your chat." Red hair and a nice voice, reassuring.

Her dress is long, too big on such a slender figure, in a soft green color, pale, like her face, the straps falling from her shoulders. She's lost more weight since last February and the heat does not help her confront her illness. A slight hint of make-up is on her cheeks and around her eyes. A glass (water, fruit juice or something else?) and a pack of cigarettes already opened lie next to an unopened one, ready for use. Hers are Virginia Circles. Short hair, burned by chemotherapy, her usual smile – melancholic and mocking. Well cared for hands, polished nails. Dignified, elegant. "I went downtown with Mirella to buy some linen clothes. Green, orange. Vibrant colors... unlike me. I've always liked them." Two pairs of large eyeglasses with dark rims lie on the table on top of a pile of scattered papers in apparent disorder.

"I asked you to come at this strange time. I wanted to prepare myself. An attractive man your age... and you show up in a brown shirt.

You look like a Nazi! I'm sorry I took you away from your family commitments."

"How are you?" – I murmur, after kissing her, afraid of embracing her, of hurting her if I hug her to me.

"You can see for yourself. Don't ask me again. You came alone. Good. I don't like to have people see me like this. What do you want to drink?"

"Water. Just water".

"Your daughter answered the phone the other day. What's she up to?"

"She's graduating from high school now, then on to study medicine."

"Medicine? Doctors? What heartless people!... But Mirella is wonderful, a real saint. If I didn't have her…"

We have addressed each other informally since the night at the Italian Consulate in New York. A privilege after having called her 'signora' for such a long time – "You know, I don't like indulging in whatever is in fashion" she explained – and you, 'Mr. Nencini'?", with her brusque ways like a sergeant. Her sight has deteriorated even more. She looks at me close-up, she needs to touch my hands continuously.

"Let's sit at the table. I'm more comfortable on the bench than on the sofa. You know, the pain in my back no longer lets me get any rest. I sleep little and badly and I'm no good for anything in the morning. I have to talk to you about a few things".

The two windows at her back overlook the street, empty and silent. It's 2:00 in the afternoon.

"Sit in front of me, on that chair" – she orders.

"Ready. I'm listening."

"I'm near the end, Riccardo, and I want to die in Florence. I told you that in New York. And now the time has come. But I'll die standing on both my feet, like Emily Brontë. I even wrote it down somewhere." Lucid.

"It's too soon to die, Oriana."

"Shut up. It'll be sometime between August and September. And I still have a lot of things to put into order. Unpleasant things, but they still need to be done. To start with, my house here in Porta Romana. There I have wonderful memories, photographs, my collections of hats and antique pocket watches that would make you green with envy. Wherever I happened to be I'd search for antique watches and mementos from the past to buy. I had a wonderful brooch from the Napoleon period.

I'd often wear it during interviews with heads of state, to inspire awe" – she laughs mischievously. "I have my clothes there, too – some of them, of course – and many war souvenirs. My knapsack from Vietnam should still be in the closet. There's a tag with the address of the Italian Embassy on it. If I had been killed or injured it was supposed to be brought there. And then notes and manuscripts of my novels. A little bit of everything".

"The house where you lived with Panagulis…".

"Yes, we were there for a long time…"

"So, in Florence…"

"Where, if not here? It's my city. I was born here, my loved ones are buried here, my people. It's here that I began to long for freedom when I didn't even know what it was. There's an indissoluble tie between Florence and myself, in spite of everything. We Fallacis are stubborn."

"I understand. You never forget the color of the earth where you've lived. Sooner or later you go back, each in his own way".

Silence suddenly and heavily descends. Right away she laid all her cards on the table without hiding anything. That's her style. The theme is death: and so be it. Giving it dignity, and not whining about memories or the golden age gone by – if ever there was one – to prepare for the final battle against cancer without giving up, without deception. Standing on both feet.

She speaks, as I always have heard her speak, with a strong Florentine accent. She does it naturally. She's never given it up. Her obsessive search for stylistic perfection in her writing is countered by her unrestrained freedom when she speaks. In her use of words, in her witty remarks, in the inflections that she indulges in and searches for, almost as if she wishes to reconciliate with her city. Straightforward.

I understood the way she was from her first phone call in October, 2002, a few weeks after the Social Forum. I was in Rome, in my car, in the pouring rain at sunset. My cell phone rang. "President Nencini, this is Oriana Fallaci and I'm calling from New York. I'd like to talk about the Social Forum." "Of course, sure. Right now I'm busy and I'm not alone. Call me tomorrow morning."

"Tomorrow morning!? You must be joking! I told you who I was. You are Nencini? Yes or no?" That was the unforgettable and unmistakable beginning.

That was Oriana.

"Can I help you?"

"Perhaps. I trust you. And I'm alone."

"So talk to me. I'm listening."

"I want to die in the Mannelli Tower, looking at the Arno River from the Ponte Vecchio. Do you know why? It was the headquarters of the partisan group my father commanded, called Giustizia e Libertà (Justice and Freedom). Actionists, liberals, socialists. I used to go there when I was a child with the nom de guerre 'Emilia'. I brought the hand grenades to the adults. I hid them in heads of lettuce. I'd take out the 'heart' of the lettuce and stick them in. Do you know what the heart is?"

"I was born in the country, too."

"All right. I'd cut the heart out of the lettuce and in its place I'd hide a bomb as big as a fist. The Allies parachuted them down in boxes on Monte Giovi, above Pontassieve, together with weapons, newspapers, chocolate and cigarettes. They were so stupid…"

"Why stupid?" – I ask.

"I'll tell you later."

I realize that as the story is flowing, she over-laps story upon story – she is like a river about to overflow – almost as if she wanted to transfer her memories – oral history – to someone else so that they won't be forgotten.

"I'd come into town – I was a young girl with braids, and my mother didn't know anything about what my father was asking me to do. God, she would have been so angry! –riding a bicycle with a basket attached to the handlebars full of fruit, vegetables and those heads of let-tuce, and head for the Mannelli Tower. At the check points the Germans hardly ever stopped me. Why would they… I was just a little girl!"

"Did you ever meet Nada Giorgi, Cassola's 'Mara' in *Bebo's Girl*...? She's two years older than you. She also shuttled between Monte Giovi and the partisan groups."

She thinks a minute. "No. I don't remember her. Is she really still alive?"

"She's a wonderful lady in her eighties. I spoke with her a few days ago. She lives in Pelago and often thinks about her Bebo."

The Mannelli family built the tower at the end of the Ponte Vecchio on the other side of the Arno River, when neither the College of the Priors nor the Rules of Justice imposed by Giano della Bella and by the middle class on the wealthy upper class Florentine merchants, existed yet. Before the towers were demolished or reduced in height – shortly after the middle of the 13th century – there were at least two hundred towers in Florence. It was a vertical city, a hexagon on the ground built around the Cardus and Decumanus but decisively pointing towards the sky. In a malevolent age, the political factions prospered by fighting and they needed fortified houses to live in, to defend themselves and to prosper. The de-

feated were exiled, stripped of all possessions, humiliated in the squares. Dante and Petraccolo di ser Parenzo, Petrarch's father, were among them. Nothing was left to chance. Especially after the Easter Sunday that stained both the Arno River and the white robe of Buondelmonte with blood. The clan, Ghibelline sympathizers and related to Uberti di Manente known as 'Farinata', shared the fate of the defeated after the battle of Benevento. They were exiled and changed their name – thus the Mannelli became the Pontigiani – and their political beliefs to become Guelphs, and finally returned to the city. The construction, the only one of the four "heads of the bridge" still standing and built during those years, should have been torn down to make place for the Vasari Corridor, but the family opposed this plan and Vasari was forced to modify his project by making the 'corridor' go around the tower.

"I want to die in that tower. I was told that you can still see the corbels in pietra serena."

"I think I know the owner, Oriana."

"You think you do or do you really know him?"

"I know him."

"So talk to him quickly. There's no time left. I have to go to Rome in a few days. From there I'm going to America to take care of a few things and then I'm coming back here. Ask him how much the rent is for a couple of months." Practical. Involved yet detached. It seems as if she's speaking about another person.

"I'll contact him tomorrow and let you know."

"Don't forget!" – she orders.

I talked with the owner. He was very gracious. The tower, however, was not fit to be lived in: there were no bedrooms, the apartment was difficult to reach and above all it seemed inadequate for a seriously ill woman. Oriana went there a few days later, she had dark glasses on, wide trousers and two bags full of objects and papers, one in her hand and one on her shoulder: a war correspondent. She hadn't been back since 1944. Moved, she gazed through the long window that looks over the river and cried. She remembered everything. Where her father waited for her, where she hid the hand grenades, the partisans getting ready for action, her naivety.

We left her alone. She could catch a glimpse of Brunelleschi's dome and of the tower, higher than any other, designed by Arnolfo di Cambio for the building that used to belong to the Foraboschi. I imagine it crossed her mind. "The Florentines are unforgiving. They erected the Palace of the Priors in a wider area that wasn't a square just so they wouldn't occupy the land which had belonged to the Uberti. Deconsecrated land. An L-shaped square came out of it, different from all the others. And to hell with Farinata who was the one who had actually saved the city after Montaperti."

"I was talking about the Allies before the liberation of Florence. They were stupid. Stupid because they put the partisans' lives at risk. They tossed fliers from the sky in Italian and newspapers in English. And what if the Germans found them? What would you tell them? That you had bought them at the news-stand in Galluzzo? Besides, who would read them? No one knew the language. Some didn't even speak Italian."

I smile, amused. "Tell me about it."

"It was in one of those newspapers that I saw the house I would buy 40 years later in New York. I liked it right away. We lived in a little house outside of the historical center. We didn't have much money and there were five of us in the family: four women – three daughters and my mum – and my dad. I remember the books. So many of them. And my father's moral strictness. That house, though, was magnificent and from the photograph it looked as if it had meadows near it, a brownstone on the East Side in Manhattan. When I went for the first time to New York I raced to see it. I was abroad for work – maybe for a war, who knows – when they told me it was for sale. I spent all my savings on it and it still wasn't enough."

Another cigarette, and another one. I smoke, too. A sip from the glass. She just wets her lips. Champagne, she says. "I hardly eat anything. I can't digest. The cancer. Champagne at least gives me some vitamins."

"Do you want to rest?"

"I've been resting all morning" – she says brusquely. "I already told you: I don't sleep. My back. Where I was wounded by splinters in Mexico City has now developed cancer."

"In Mexico City?"

"Right. For work. It was October, 1968, the eve of the Olympics, and a student protest was going on, something they had never seen before. The students were protesting because the games were a waste of money. The military had surrounded the UNAM campus and they were about to occupy it. I heard the whirring of the helicopters coming closer. The students, hundreds of them, many barricaded in a building in the Three Cultures Square, raised their eyes to the sky. I also turned. The sound reminded me of the American helicopters in Vietnam. A bad sign…"

She tells it as if the scene were right in front of her, alive, and uses her hands to describe it, her voice gloomy, intense.

"… Get down, get down!" – I yelled. They didn't understand what was happening. The confusion covered the first shots. A massacre. They started shooting from everywhere and we were trapped in a cul-de-sac. Tanks, machine guns, rifles. I saw a small baby, really small, with its head blown off by machine gun fire, and another that was running… running… running… cut in half by the shots.

The wounds on my back are a souvenir of that day. They thought I was dead, they took me to the morgue and they threw me on top of a pile of corpses. Blood was everywhere. Just imagine… a priest realized that I was still alive". Silence. "The worst slaughter I ever saw.

Nebiolo (*editor's note,* Gino Nebiolo a colleague and friend) came to the hospital with a photographer and I dictated my piece to him while I was lying in the bed."

A cigarette. A glass. She glances at a book, lifts it from the table and turns it over in her hands. "Don Milani. Neera, my sister, wrote it. She's an excellent writer. The best of us because all three of us write. I would have liked to prepare a new edition." A hand gesture as if to say "I can no longer do it."

"Listen, Riccardo, poverty taught me many things, war did the rest. Not even in Vietnam did I see massacres like the one in Mexico. I saw war when I was a child. I remember my father being taken away and tortured in Villa Triste, the fliers I would paste on walls when I was a young girl during the occupation of Florence, the dire poverty then, and the good people that helped each other. My mother didn't know anything about those fliers that I pasted advocating the end of the war. How irresponsible my father was!… What if the Germans or the Fascists had caught me?"

"You must have been pretty. A beautiful face…"

"Skinny, my God, I was so skinny! Listen. One day dad sent me without my mother knowing – it must have been the beginning or maybe the spring of 1944 – to Piazza Pitti to bring Carlo Levi a revolver and something to eat, right in front of the palace, in the open. I was fourteen. He lived in a room full of books and paintings. He was a sad man, not very talkative. I had put everything in a bundle. He opened it and do you know what he said to me? This is a ladies' revolver – as if one had a choice in those days! – I don't want it, and the things you brought me to eat… isn't there anything else? I answered that we hardly had anything to eat ourselves because we had to put food aside for him and others like him. He made me take the revolver back. With the Germans positioned right there nearby! They had piled up hundreds of works of art in Palazzo Pitti."

A native of Turin, Carlo Levi was connected to the Giustizia e Libertà movement. A friend of Carlo and Nello Rosselli, he returned to Italy from France in 1943 after years of internment, and in December he rented a room in the boarding house owned by Anna Maria Ichino in Piazza Pitti.

He stayed there until August 1945. In 1944 he became associate editor of the "Nazione del Popolo". He wrote Christ Stopped at Eboli in that room and painted his most important works. During those dramatic years a remarkable coterie of free minds met in Ms. Ichino's house: Manlio Cancogni, Natalia Ginzburg, Cecchi and Montale, Bilenchi and Mario Luzi. Umberto Saba moved in after September 8th, 1943.

"At my funeral, I would like a cannon salvo. When I was 14 – the war had just ended – General Alexander, head of the Allied Forces in Italy, awarded me a Diploma of Honor. The story of the lettuce without the heart and a few hours spent as a lookout…"

Her illness hasn't devoured her memory. The details now flow non-stop as she talks about her interviews with the powerful of the world: the kiss to Deng Xiaoping and the portrait of Mao in Tiananmen Square in Beijing, the ire of Kissinger, the movements of Qaddafi in the desert, Khomeini and the chador taken off during the interview, her friendship with Pietro Nenni, her esteem for the ascetic and aristocratic Enrico Berlinguer. She remembers everything with pride.

"After wars, peace never comes straightaway. Never. Revenge, slander, betrayal, accusations against others – they are all the order of the day. It happened also in Florence, in 1945. One evening, my uncle Bruno came to our house after witnessing the execution of a sniper in Piazza Santa Maria Novella. The young man had put a cigarette in his mouth, stepped over the corpses of his fascist comrades and, with a cocky air, waited to die. I saw similar scenes in Vietnam, in the Middle East, wherever there had been war. I saw cowardly and courageous men together… The same thing happens when political regimes fall. At Porta Romana there were German soldiers who wanted to give themselves up, and others who continued to loot houses and the few shops that were still open. Later, a sinister calm descended…" She is quiet all of a sudden. Reflecting. "By the way" – she asks – "do you know what happened to the Vietnamese police chief – his name was Loan – who, in cold blood, shot a Vietcong prisoner in the head on a street in Saigon?…

The one in the photo that was seen all over the world and published in lots of books… a pistol pointed at his head and boom… right in front of the camera! That photo had a devastating effect on public opinion. The general escaped to the United States in 1975, he went to Virginia and opened a restaurant. Imagine, a restaurant."

It was February 1ˢᵗ, 1968. The prisoner was executed by General Nguyen Ngoc Loan in front of an NBC cameraman and a photographer, Eddie Adams. The photo won the Pulitzer Prize in 1969. The image immediately became a pacifist icon. An interview with General Loan is included in Nothing, and So Be It.

"I was already old enough to remember what dad said, then one morning – I was with my mum in Borgo Pinti – we saw a group of five or six men who were tormenting a girl. 'Fascist, fascist whore!' – they were yelling while they beat her in the middle of the street. My mother went up to them and pulled her away from them. 'I've already cried for my husband, beaten up by the Carità gang – she railed as I had never seen her do before – 'that's enough'. She never was a fascist, the girl I mean, or at least no more than other Florentines and Italians were. She had become a prostitute in order to feed her two children. A poor wretch before, a poor wretch now. All that in a city that had once been truly fascist and then, when the war was over, had suddenly become totally antifascist."

"There were many people, the majority, who changed sides when everything was over, when the Allied tanks were already in the south of Tuscany, but who nonetheless had a hard time. Immediately after September 8th, 1943, those who had gone into the mountains or had organized the Resistance Movement in the cities had to make an even more difficult choice."

"Much more difficult! At Ponte alla Mosse – Florence had only recently been liberated, snipers were still on the rooftops – an event occurred that tells a lot about turncoats, the wife of a former fascist officer was beating chained German prisoners. My mother railed against her vehemently…" Pause. "And you should have heard my dad and the few others like him, who really had participated in the Resistance!"

"The same thing also happened elsewhere. Do you remember Flaiano and his talking about jumping on the bandwagon of the victors?"

"The expression isn't his. Whose is it... whose is it? He also wrote it but he got it from someone else. From... from..."

She takes off her glasses and lifts a hand to her right eye. I pour some water for her. I get up so she won't feel embarrassed.

"Please. Sit down. Do I bother you?"

"I'm sorry. You still have such beautiful eyes." Her eyes. Piercing, enquiring, curious.

"Stop it. I promised you in February that I would do some research on Ippolita degli Azzi. I don't like being compared to someone without knowing who they are."

When the gold medal was awarded to her at the Italian Consulate in New York in February 2006, we compared Oriana's story with that of Ippolita degli Azzi. It piqued her curiosity and she decided to find out more about this woman who was so special.

"She was courageous and, for her time, a maverick. She had little in common with women her age and with Medieval women in general. First of all she knew how to read and write. She steadfastly opposed her father's decision to have her marry a man she did not love. But that was the practice then and it went on for a long time."

The pain has become sharp. She stands up and leans on the window sill with her hands. It's 4:30. The heat is oppressive, suffocating and deadly like the cavalry maneuvers led by the Carthaginian commander Hannibal at Cannae.

Ippolita degli Azzi, born in Arezzo and from a noble Ghibelline family, defended the walls of Arezzo after the Guelph army victory in Campaldino. Out of contempt for the defeated, the Florentines catapulted donkeys with miters over the city's bastions after the palio (horse race). *Arezzo didn't fall and she became a symbol of resistance and courage. Legend says she was very beautiful, an indomitable amazon, yet prisoner of a hopeless love. Oriana, too, if she had to choose between the Guelphs and Ghibellines, would have taken the side of the latter without hesitation. Knights with a code of honor, not petty merchants attracted by 'quick profits' and ready to betray.*

"I've been having radiation therapy once or twice a week since the beginning of the year, sometimes three times." She glances at her hands. "The treatments don't do much good. They make me befuddled and they torment me." She sits with her back straight, erect.

"By the way, thanks for your book. Who knows if I'll read it…"

"You had me give it to you and now you're not going to read it? That's rude…"

She gazes intensely at me without commenting. Blue eyes.

"Right. But I have something for you, too. I found it at the Argosy Bookstore on East 59th. It's a book on current events.

" She goes and gets it. A precious edition of *The Rape of the Bucket* by Tassoni, "a heroic-comic poem" – she points out mischievously.

"It's magnificent. Thank you. Thanks with all my heart, Oriana."

"You too collect antique books, don't you?"

"Yes, for a few years. I inherited some nice volumes from my grandparents, mostly veterinary books."

"Look here. There's a typographical error on the front cover. The year 1806. Naturally they mean 2006. Isn't it obvious? Unless Vico was actually right, as well as the proverb that goes: 'Everything changes and goes back to what it was before'. Ah, I'd have loved to be in Italy in spring. This government won't last, but before it falls we'll see some fine messes. Easy for you to say, Cassandra."

A smug smile plays on her lips. I make no comment. I listen and think: "She's not all wrong."

Another cigarette. She offers me one. I take it. We smoke without speaking. She leafs through papers lying on the table and I look at a lithograph hanging on the wall to her right.

"On June 12th in Bergamo I was put on trial for the 'crime of opinion'. Sorry: defamation of Islam. A trial sought by the Muslim who tosses crucifixes out the window and who still sells the worthless book *Islam Punishes Oriana Fallaci*. Have you ever read it?"

"No. I don't have time for libelers. A few months ago the Regional Council approved a motion to express their solidarity with you." It hadn't been easy, I told her. On the contrary. After a heated discussion – the motion had been presented by the councilor Pieraldo Ciucchi – finally the Assembly voted strongly in favor of it. It was the first time that a debate about freedom of opinion, but actually based on the 'Fallaci affair', had ended with the support of the regional parliament.

"Calling on the four Suras of the Koran, our dear Adel Smith invites his brothers to murder me, but no magistrate has brought him to trial for instigation to murder."

The accusation of defamation of the Islamic religion was based on eighteen sentences contained in The Force of Reason. *The hearing on June 12th had been adjourned until the 26th of the same month. At that session, Judge Beatrice Siccardi had allowed Adel Smith – president of the Union of Muslims in Italy, whose charge had started the proceedings – to sue her for damages.*

The public prosecutor Carmen Pugliese up-held the charge after having taken the place of Maria Cristina Rota, who asked to be replaced after her request to dismiss the charge had been rejected during the first hearing. The trial was again adjourned until December 18th, but Oriana had already passed away. The reason was formal: "… we cannot proceed due to the death of the offender."

I try to change the subject, going around the same theme. I know the danger but, like a moth attracted to a flame, I can't back away. On a windy and cold night in New York, piles of snow between the trees and on the street corners, we had discussed at length and argued about the weak values of the West and the pervasive and oppressive strength of Islam. The consul, Bandini, became alarmed and upon my request to continue the exchange of opinions in a secluded room, he diplomatically exclaimed: "Slit your own throats, if you like". Now she circles around the matter before facing up to it. And so I do it.

"After September 11th, you became convinced that the crisis in the West had opened the doors to the Islamic threat and that this process is irreversible. The Church now has become a bulwark, the source from which to draw values and certainties. Or rather, the only mainstay."

"And you don't agree."

"No, I don't agree. I listen to you when you talk about the crisis of values in our society but I disagree when you think the Church is the sole repository of the tools needed to stand up to, what you define as, the Islamic offensive, and your opinion on the illiberality of a Koranic religion that has now become a State, makes me think that... standing up to an Islam steeped in fundamentalism by relying mainly on another religion, setting the Koran against the Bible and the Gospels and totally disregarding the secular values of Europe, is not the right way."

She replies with a calm voice, as if she were discussing an already-proven theory. No complications. Everything is right in front of us, plain as can be.

"Riccardo, the West is sick, it's lost its will to fight, it opposes Islamic fundamentalism with empty values. The West is fat and they're hungry, we no longer have a faith and they do. Europe has become spineless. All we need now is for a golden bridge to be built when Turkey enters the European Union."

"It's not just religious values, for God's sake" – her voice rises. "Moral goodness isn't just Christian; the 'good' principles are not always the ones you invoke, Oriana. You've spent your life trying to prove the contrary!"

"Spineless, Europe has become spineless. Freedom has become permissiveness and if you write that, a gang of intellectuals" – she pronounces 'intellectuals' with a clear scorn – "will be ready to jump on you". The end.

"I still have so much to do and instead I have to get ready to leave this world. Those things that I've never taken much into consideration, to tell you the truth. Copyright, my will, my business with Rizzoli. And then there's my family, what's left of my family. I've written many pages on the history of the Fallacis. Grandparents, great-grandparents, ancestors going back to the 18th century. But I'm not finished yet. Not much left, maybe the last chapter."

She rests her hand on a pile of papers, a compact block of typewritten papers some twenty-five centimeters high. I look at the reams of paper without speaking. The fruit of ten years work interrupted by the attack on the Twin Towers. She protects it as she would do with a newborn baby. I catch a glimpse of the title written in pen but I can't read it because her splayed fingers cover it, fingers that every once in a while drum on the top of the pile of papers. She notices my curiosity but doesn't acknowledge it. I move with caution.

"A Family Saga."

"What makes you think that? I've always loved the Greve countryside and the Chianti. The Fallacis come from there, from Panzano. It was my duty to buy that house."

"Roots. I feel them deeply, too. You for Chianti and I for the Mugello. Did you know the family of Leonardo's Mona Lisa came from your parts?"

"Ah, really? Who said so?" She looks at me suspiciously but attentively.

"Giuseppe Pallanti, a Florentine scholar. An impressive work of research still not finished. Lisa was a Gherardini who married a Del Giocondo. The mystery was revealed after specific documents were found in the convent of Sant'Orsola in Florence. You have the same roots. They go deep into the vineyards of Chianti... and both of you were born in June! The most famous women in Italy both have blood from Greve..."

"Listen to that... the Mona Lisa, too... Roots – and a bit of courage I must say – kept me company in Da Nang and in the rice paddies of Vietnam, during the nights illuminated by fires in the Middle East, under the cannon fire and amidst people shot down by machine guns. Maybe they also helped me in making my decisions. One day we were supposed to get on an airplane to go into a war zone, miles away from Saigon. I said to a colleague... I don't remember who... no, I'm not taking that plane. Thank God. It never arrived."

"Cassandra."

"Luck, instinct, who knows. I got used to making quick decisions. When you're in a trench, in a hole with soldiers that are dying next to you, you have to be quick. Now it's easier. There are other means, satellite phones, and computers. There are war correspondents that do their reports from four-star hotel rooms. They look out from their terrace with a cup of tea in their hand and what do they see? The swimming pool or the garden. Still they write. And what pieces! Well, even back then some people used the same technique. I never did."

After having been a journalist during the Hungarian insurrection, Oriana, war correspondent for the magazine "Europeo", went to Vietnam for the first time in 1967. She went back twelve times in seven years, staying for endless weeks and writing, without sparing anyone her criticism, extremely well-documented and uncomfortable stories and articles. As a correspondent, she also followed the conflict between India and Pakistan, the wars in the Middle East and the countless episodes of guerilla warfare in South America. And finally, the Gulf War and the entry of the American troops into Kuwait City. She expressed praise for Giovanna Botteri, the RAI correspondent in Iraq: "She has a haunted look but a calm voice. With the tanks rattling next to you it isn't easy to keep calm."

"Don't leave. Wait a minute."

She stands up again, cursing the heat and leaves the dining room. I take Neera's book in my hands and glance through it.

How many volumes have been written about Don Milani after his death and how many theses credited to him! Too many by those who have never read a passage he wrote, the same number by those who twisted his thoughts to adapt them politically to one side. I've met many young people who passed through Barbiana and are now

adults. Most of them, educated at his church, be-
came members of the Socialist Party in Vicchio or
in Calenzano. Recently I read again Letter to a
Teacher. *I had a vague, but clear memory of it to*
put into perspective an excess of clichés around
which flowered an unbearable rhetoric. An inno-
vator in education and at the same time an enemy
of modernity and merit. A forerunner of '68 and
a tenacious opponent of every type of knowledge
that wasn't tied to everyday life experiences. Why
see him still today as a model educator? Why con-
sider him a master of today's school in Italy?

She comes back and is more relaxed.

"Two abortions. If I hadn't led such a life… Do you have children? Yes, yes, I remember the dedication I wrote for… What's her name?"

"Giulia, the eldest. Classical studies at Galileo High School and then medical school, like you…"

"Medicine! What a mistake, what a mistake! Tell her to change her mind."

"I wouldn't even try. She's so convinced. Then I have a boy and a girl, Mattia and Ricciarda."

"Three children! You're a lucky man. What wonderful names they have…"

"They're very sweet and loving kids."

"Tough luck for them. Life doesn't reward feelings. I've experienced hunger, fear, war and I started working very young. It's made me hard but I had no other choice. Did you at least teach them manners?"

"The boy pours out drinks for his sisters and opens the door for ladies…"

"Good, good. That's the way it should be. You know, I am a bit of an old-fashioned revolutionary."

She stops talking.

"Do you know how I came to write '*Letter to a Child Never Born*'?"

"I've heard a couple of versions…"

"But maybe you don't know the true one. The editor of *Europeo* had commissioned me to write a series of articles – an investigation – on abortion in Italy. I had only a few weeks to deliver them. I showed up right on time with the typewritten copy of the book. 'And·where are the pieces to be published?' – he yelled, turning purple. 'There aren't any' – I replied. Pandemonium broke out…"

We have been talking for four hours non-stop. She's serene. Irksome and difficult when we venture into issues and people she doesn't like, but she doesn't turn bitter. She's strangely calm even in her opinions except when the conversation turns to politicians – with no exceptions – and to fellow journalists. Biting, ironic, harsh. Is she approaching death knowingly, like Hector accepting Achilles' challenge, she who has always loved life and feared death above all else? I don't know. I don't sense fear, though, behind her words. Perhaps disappointment and frustration for the work that will remain unfinished, projects matured over time and abandoned on the bookshelves of her house on the Upper East Side or in her head waiting to be hatched. She's told me more than once that living without being able to read freely makes no sense. She can't bear it.

"I work to defeat the alien" – she yelled at me ever since our very first phone calls between the two continents – "because right now it would be wrong to keep quiet."

"I'm about to die" – she murmurs more than once, but she doesn't talk about death. She orders how her – strictly private – funeral should be organized, in the Allori cemetery, next to her father, mother, sister and to Panagulis' memorial stone – and decides who is allowed to attend it – hardly anyone, let alone politicians and detractors with their crocodile tears. "I've never liked sycophants and cowards. On the other hand I've always been irreverent towards powerful people." Nothing more.

"I've worked a lot in my life. Sixty years. And I've never become rich."

"You made a good living and you did what you wanted. You were lucky. Like me."

"Lucky… Do you know how much someone who writes for a daily newspaper earns today? There's no comparison."

Pause.

"I have to go back to New York. The house is full of papers, books, notes…"

"If we set up a foundation dedicated to you in the *Biblioteca per l'Identità Toscana* or in the *Fondazione del Consiglio Regionale*, you could donate some of your writings, your books, and the objects that accompanied you on your missions. With our commitment to make it accessible to the public for study purposes. You would be in good company because Mario Luzi's papers will soon be there."

"And after you, who would manage it?"

"I wouldn't manage it myself. It would belong to the Regional Council."

"Can they be trusted?"

"Of course."

"I'll have to think about it" – she ends curtly.

"Oriana, don't forget about it. You would make your city and region happy. We already asked you once, four years ago, to participate in a Festival of Tuscany (November 30th of each year, in remembrance of the abrogation of torture and death penalty by the Grand Duke in 1786, *editor's note)* and you declined the invitation."

"How could I come?… The Muslims would have paid all the money in the world to do me in." She raises her hand in the air with a couldn't-care-less gesture.

"And does my city deserve it?" Like a cat with a mouse in its mouth, Oriana doesn't attack me, nor spew curses. She remembers a meeting years ago with the mayor and his wife. She doesn't comment and lights a new cigarette but at the wrong end. I take it from her hands, put it out and offer her one of mine. All of a sudden, her invective. Calm, lucid, resolute, concise.

"Do you know who wrote the harshest opinions about our dear, little Florence? Do you know? Tiziano Terzani. He was much more critical towards the city administrators than I ever was. He who praised Maoism…"

She rummages among the papers spread on the table until she pulls out a letter.

"Read!" – she orders. "Out loud so you remember it."

Readable handwriting. Thank God. The signature is Terzani's. The date: September, 2001.

"And yet one day politics will have to rejoin with ethics if we want to live in a better world…"

"Keep going, dear."

"… this city hurts me and makes me sad. Everything has changed, everything has become vulgar…"

"Perfect. Keep going, Riccardo."

"… but the fault is not with Islam and the immigrants. They aren't the ones who made Florence into a town of merchants prostituting itself to tourism. Florence was beautiful when it was smaller and poorer. Now it's a disgrace… Believe me, I feel out of place here myself, too."

"Period."

She smiles mischievously like a poker player touched by Lady Luck.

"You were offensive. It was a personal attack…" She doesn't let me finish.

"… That Japanese's metal structure and the Social Forum…" – she smiles with satisfaction. "But I had discussed it with everyone beforehand. With everyone, you understand! The prefect, the Home Secretary, even with Fassino and others I won't name. Only my anarchist friends from Carrara were missing from the list. As for the 'canopy' by that Japanese… what's his name?"

"Isozaki… His name is Isozaki."

"… I talked about it with Ms. Petrioli Tofani (former director of the Uffizi Gallery, *editor's note*) and she talked to me about Paolucci (the then superintendent for the Department of Florentine Museums, *editor's note*) and they all talked to me about Urbani (the then Minister for Arts and Culture, *editor's note*) The result: who knows! As it often happens in Florence: the hot potato is passed around. If the ancient priors and the *boni homini* (good men) that met in San Pier Scheraggio to decide where to build the Duomo and Palazzo Vecchio had seen us, they would have thought: what jerks!"

"Different roles, Oriana."

"Of course…" Skeptical.

"Even Montanelli, another contrary person like you, didn't have any praise for Florence. Last year we published, together with the Fucecchio Foundation, a humorous little history book with a different point of view called, *La Mia Firenze*. Montanelli even dates the crisis as far back as the 16th century when the Florentine merchants began buying titles of nobility and living on their income. Instead of being proud of themselves, the merchants wanted to become part of the old ruling class, the aristocracy. This tendency to 'Hispanicize' was introduced under Cosimo to attract the young men who scorned commerce into the Order of St. Stephen. Goodbye to entrepreneurial spirit and innovation. It all ended up with splendidly decorated coats of arms, and marquises and counts suffering from gout." She laughs with satisfaction.

"You see? At least they built palaces and had them frescoed, they donated sculptures and paintings to churches, built hospitals and brought wealth to the city. The most generous patrons lived there and they hired the best artists of the time. But today? Nothing new has been built and the historical center is in such a state! Everyone cleaned their portion of the street then. Now they don't even empty the litter bins."

"Eleven million tourists a year, Oriana."

"So what? Did they close the website 'Nencinithinkaboutitagain@yahoo.it'?"

"A long time ago. Goal made, game over."

In the late afternoon, when the sunset announces itself with an explosion of red and a wisp of wind scarcely moves the leaves on the motionless trees, Oriana stands up again. She's tired. I smoked too much but the ashtray in front of me doesn't compare to hers. It overflows with cigarette ash and butts. She looks out one of the two windows after throwing open the shutters. The guards – mine – wander about the cars.

"Poor things, they've been there since 2:00?"

"Yes"– I reply, stretching my legs.

"At least I'd make coffee for mine at night. Carabinieri?"

"Yes, loyal till the end of time. They've followed me around for five years. Good people. They eat with me, too. Mostly sandwiches. We're always in a rush."

"They're the best. They're disciplined and they don't betray you."

They notice her, a small figure in the window. They wave to her and she waves back. The street, silent, simmers with heat. A man wearing sandals turns the corner and quickly heads away.

"What time is it?" – she asks me.

"Almost 7:00. Do you want to eat something or would you rather rest a while?"

"Eat? And how could I do that with cancer…" – she touches her chest. "No, I don't even want to sleep. Maybe you're the one who has to leave…"

"I have nothing I need to do and I'm fine here with you."

Silence. Both of us are seized by an unexpected, sudden wave of melancholy. It's at that moment that the illness shows itself with its greatest strength, when words cease and defeat presents itself as the only possible certainty. Oriana uses words to defend herself, to protect herself from the tumor – or rather, the tumors – in order to forget. She struggles, as she always has, to push solitude and death further away. She is not proud, now, of her solitude, she doesn't flaunt it as if it were a banner of virtue, the oriflamme against every impurity.

She is standing in front of the wide open window, a fistful of nerves without flesh. Sweet, fragile, defenseless. The siege is over, the enemy has conquered the keep and is about to pour inside the walls. It will take no prisoners.

Oriana realizes now how long this moment has been, and so the soldier in her reappears, disciplined even though the scars of the wars fought are all carved on her body. Neither the haughty and braggart soldier – Pyrgopolynices was his name – created by the imagination of Plautus, nor the mercenary, enlisted by a constable into the service of any seigniory. A testy but trustworthy foot soldier, the mainstay of the century, short-tempered, impossible but fearless, generous behind the sullen face of one who was brought up for war, an elitist like one who is used to fighting crucial battles but not futile skirmishes.

Like a foot soldier in the republican army who takes care of his weapons, Oriana is a perfectionist with the written word. She detests rhyme, assonance, sentences built with words having the same sound. Every page is the result of an effort repeated a hundredfold: the search for synonyms, scholarly and unusual citations, preparation by reading innumerable texts. And always in complete silence. In silence and solitude.

I've always doubted that Oriana was a woman alone. She prefers solitude but she is neither lonesome nor isolated from the world.

In the residence of Consul Bandini in Manhattan, in the presence of Riccardo Mazzoni, Gianluca Parrini and Angelo Pollina, she articulated clearly with her voice hoarsened by nicotine: "Man ist allein mit allem, was man liebt" (Man is alone with everything that he loves). We had asked her about Panagulis. She answered that she had never been unfaithful to him when he was alive and not even after his death. An everlasting love, in spite of his mother. As it should be, she pointed out with obstinate passion while looking into our eyes. Novalis' quotation was dropped there and then.

Ippolita degli Azzi, I think, with her hope-less love for Rinaldo de' Bostoli, a Guelph in a Ghibelline city before the drama of Romeo and Juliet. Arezzo, therefore, not yet Shakespeare's Verona.

Then, suddenly I remember. The question: to ask or not to ask? By asking, do I violate her privacy or cause her pain?

"What are you thinking about? I can see the wheels turning."

"You've always spoken about Panagulis, on-ly about Panagulis..."

"But there was François Pelou, the director of France-Presse in Saigon, too. What an attrac-tive man! Do you know how it ended?"

"I don't even know how it began, Oriana."

"A stormy argument, the last, maybe in Madrid. He had decided not to divorce. I made a package of the letters we had exchanged and I sent them to his wife. Amen. We never saw each other again. Never again."

Ippolita's family descended from the Ober-tenghis of Tuscia, marquises of Lombard origins from whom also came the marquises of Canossa and the Este dynasty of Ferrara. Consular nobility that, at the end of the 13th century, became related to the rich and powerful Ubertini family. I like to think, as the legend goes, that Ippolita saw Rinaldo again, after he was exiled by the bishop-lord of Arezzo, Guglielmino degli Ubertini, riding around the crenellated bastions of her city which was under siege by the Florentines. The summer of 1289 had just begun and Rinaldo, having joined the Guelph army, was fighting at the side of her enemies. I tried to imagine Ippolita's pain and solitude during those bloody days: the husband her father had forced her to marry, had died in battle at Campaldino; the man she loved and who returned her love was siding with the enemy; and she herself, paradoxically under close watch by the defenders of Arezzo, those who feared betrayals, just when she had decided to risk her life for them. Ippolita chose her destiny and remained faithful to it until the end. Neither woman, ever alone. Simply lovers of solitude after having found and recognized fate along the way.

"I'll fix you something for dinner. In New York you preferred crap to my cooking. You've never had my pancakes."

"Don't worry. In this heat I only feel like eating fruit and ice cream. Mirella will be back soon."

"Your kids. Where are your kids?"

"Out and about, I think. Giulia is probably studying her Greek. She has her oral exams in a few days."

"Remind me to give you two hats for the girls… You know, I would have wanted to continue *Letter to a Child Never Born*. It's a hymn to life even if the title might be misleading. Have you read it? It's not just a women's book."

"On the plane coming back to Italy from your other city. The copy with your dedication. The first time, though, while I was at university."

"Do you usually read the same book twice?"

"Rarely, but it happens. A different age, a different sensibility, more knowledge."

"I don't know how many times I've left Italy only to come back. I really don't know. Anyway, Italy has never especially cared for me… Last year Ciampi sent me a bunch of flowers with a card, a very nice card. It was after the award given to me by him as the President of the Italian Republic. I asked Monsignor Fisichella to do me the courtesy of picking it up for me. In New York I frequently see Isabella Rossellini. She loves my cooking, as do her children. Sophia Loren often calls me – what a woman!… She raised her two children without giving up her profession – and I've kept up a good relationship with Zeffirelli. Once, I showed up uninvited at a première in New York. They didn't want to let me in and they were right. 'Call the director' – I said. 'Do you know the maestro?' Amazed and admiring. 'Tell him that Oriana's here'. He arrived out of breath". A gust of wind.

"I'll get you some plums. Come on, a big man like you…"

"No. I'm fine."

"Italy hasn't cared for me, but Italians have. They've read my works more than those of any other woman writer. Do you know which female Italians are the most well known in the world? Eleonora Duse and me. That's all." Vanity.

We were supposed to discuss tedious bureaucratic matters but presently, like a stormy sea, the waves are leaving all kinds of things on the beach. Misunderstandings, old conflicts, little secrets, matters that were lost within bigger matters. I don't ask. I don't want to violate her privacy. I wait to let her decide the right time and subjects. Oscar Wilde wrote: "Moderation is a fatal thing". Oriana never ran the risk of belonging to the class of people who don't speak their minds, convinced as they are that, in order to have a better life, you have to be liked by everyone. The only god I think she devoted herself to was freedom. "And all in war with time for love of you...", if we can borrow the great Bard of Avon's quotation. " A duty more than a right", she wrote. As she speaks I remind her of a verse by Dante: "Supreme of gifts, which God creating gave Of his free bounty, […] Was liberty of will" Free will, she answers, coming close enough to brush my face. A canto from the *Paradiso*.

Cultured, biting, always outside the box, troublesome, the top of her class from the time she was little – she reminds me – and as such, set off along the road of being disliked. But not in this long, scorching afternoon. A short invective and that's all, a solitary story of a life dedicated to the typewriter and to adventure. "I can't live, I wouldn't have known how to live without adventure. Whatever happens to me I make it into a challenge. And journalism has given me plenty of adventures. But none have come without a price, every one of them has cost me dearly…"

"For every decision you make there is a price to pay" – I butt in.

"Right. But not everyone is willing to choose".

"Right".

Those who haven't had the good fortune to know her personally can't appreciate her sweetness or her frequent acts of generosity. A simple sweetness, 'masculine', disguised by brusque manners, direct. She knows the value of gratitude and she uses it as soon as her defenses are lowered, when she's made the decision to trust someone.

So, no superficial judgments, at least not to incur the harsh warning by Balzac: "to know merely the outward events of a man's life would only serve to make a chronological table — a fool's notion of history."

EPILOGUE

"Bye, Riccardo, thanks for your company. I don't know if we'll see each other again. I've gotten so much worse that the Sloan Cancer Center has raised the white flag and soon I will too. It's over. This is the end of the road. And whatever happens, have a good life".

A hug, as if we were retired comrades-in-arms. No tears.

The road is deserted. A stray dog wags its tail heading for a garbage can.

Oriana stayed in Florence only a few more days, at most a couple of weeks. Almost no one knew about it.

After being deeply moved while looking out the window of the Mannelli Tower, she visited other houses accompanied by a handful of friends, always the same ones. It was impossible to find three rooms to rent for a few months.

They looked along the river, Borgo San Iacopo with its ancient residences belonging to the Belfredelli, the Marsili and the Angiolieri families, Piazza della Signoria. The few people who had been told asked friends and acquaintances and always met with kindness and helpfulness, but the conditions she set down – the Arno, the Dome, Palazzo Vecchio, only three months, a room that had to be equipped for a seriously ill woman – and the short time they had, made the objective more and more difficult to reach as the days passed. Nothing at all. Plenty of houses to rent, or to buy, but without the cherished symbols of Florence in the background.

Oriana would go out in the torrid heat of the morning and wandering around she made peace with the alleys, the corners, the streets, the palaces, and the squares. "New York is a city that is half-home, Florence is my true home". A grey suit and hat – beret with a rim. Cigarettellos – small New York cigars wrapped in brown paper – always in her mouth. Water strictly at room temperature, not sparkling. "It is the Alien that dehydrates me. A stupid illness, you know. It will die when I die. Both of us defeated!"

My last memory is of a grey linen dress, her blue eyes hidden behind large sunglasses, a straw hat, two bags, an orange juice and a lit cigarette. "I don't want to deprive myself of bad habits". Then Rome, New York and finally Florence.

Welcome home.

ORIANA FALLACI
Biographical notes

Oriana Fallaci was born in Florence in 1929. At only sixteen she began her career in newspapers as a court reporter for the "Mattino dell'Italia Centrale". Three years later she began her collaboration with the weekly magazine "L'Europeo", where she would soon become a special correspondent.

That is the beginning of her famous news coverage that would soon make her figure among the most important names in international journalism. Since then her life would become a source for news and legend.

In 1965 Oriana Fallaci dedicated to her father the book *If the Sun Dies,* where she describes the preparations for the American landing on the moon. To write the book she met the project head of the mission, the former Nazi scientist Wernher von Braun, who had designed the V2 rockets that Hitler fired on London. In 1967 she went to Vietnam as a war correspondent and returned there 12 times in 7 years to write about the war, documenting the atrocities and heroism of both the opposing armies and writing a news-diary report that is considered her first great book, *Nothing, and So Be It.* On October 2nd, 1968, on the eve of the Olympic Games, during a Mexican university student protest march against the military occupation of the UNAM campus, today remembered as the Tlatelolco massacre, Fallaci was seriously injured. Hundreds of youths were killed and the journalist was also believed to be dead and taken to the morgue: only there did a priest realize that she was, instead, still alive.

As a correspondent she was present in all the other theaters of war including the Gulf conflict and the insurrections in Latin America.

In 1975, *Letter to a Child Never Born* was published. It was the writer's first big publishing success and the book sold four and a half million copies all over the world. After her work as a reporter she then interviewed internationally known politicians, including Ayatollah Khomeini during whose interview she called him a "tyrant" and also removed the *chador* that she had been forced to wear to be admitted in his presence. All these interviews then were collected in the book *Interview with History.*

Her masterpiece, however, is considered the novel *A Man,* about the death of Alexandros Panagulis, Fallaci's life companion and hero of the Greek resistance. Panagulis was assassinated and Fallaci begins the book with the description of the tumultuous funeral procession in which thousands upon thousands of people participated.

After her new literary work *In'shallah* was published, Oriana Fallaci moved to New York, isolating herself from everyone. There she sporadically published in newspapers her angry and sharp articles on the most burning issues of current politics.

After the attacks on September 11th, 2001 and the diagnosis of cancer, she wrote the controversial and much-discussed trilogy on Islam and the roots of the West: *The Rage and the Pride*, 2001; *The Force of Reason*, 2004; *Oriana Fallaci Interviews Herself. The Apocalypse*, 2004.

She died on September 15th, 2006 in Florence where she is buried in the Allori cemetery.

Finito di stampare in Firenze
presso la tipografia editrice Polistampa
nella tiratura limitata di 100 copie
Ottobre 2008